IT'S ALL A MATTER OF
ATTITUDE

Justin Herald

ALLEN&UNWIN

First South Asian Edition 2007
Reprinted 2008, 2009, 2010, 2011

Allen & Unwin
83 Alexander Street
Crows Nest NSW 2065
Australia
Phone: (61 2) 8425 0100
Fax: (61 2) 9906 2218
Email: info@allenandunwin.com
Web: www.allenandunwin.com

National Library of Australia
Cataloguing-in-Publication entry:

> Herald, Justin
> It's all a matter of attitude.

ISBN : 978-1-74114-497-0

This edition is licensed for sale in the Indian subcontinent only. Not for export elsewhere.

1. Self-actualisation (Psychology). 2. Success. 3. Motivation (Psychology). 4. Self-confidence. I. Title.

158.1

Printed and bound at Chennai Micro Print (P) Ltd., Export Division, 100% EOU, 130, Nelson Manickam Road, Aminjikarai, Chennai - 29 (India).

This book is dedicated to my beautiful wife, Vanessa.
Thank you for being my partner on this journey we call life.

Justin Herald is renowned for taking Attitude Inc®—the company he founded with only A$50—to international success. He is currently regarded as one of the rising stars in the fields of life improvement and personal development. He speaks to audiences all over the world motivating and inspiring them to achieve all that they desire.

He is currently the 'International Entrepreneur of the Year' and is a best-selling author of two previous books: *Would you like Attitude with that?* and *What are you waiting for?*

Justin also has numerous motivational CDs and DVDs available through his website: http://www.justinherald.com

Most people are aware that this is the slogan that launched the Attitude Gear® brand. But it is more than just a slogan; it's a way of thinking. No matter what comes your way, your attitude will be the key to handling everything.

In my first book I described the results of your attitudes this way:

POSITIVE ATTITUDE = POSITIVE RESULTS
NEGATIVE ATTITUDE = NEGATIVE RESULTS
NEUTRAL ATTITUDE = NEUTRAL RESULTS

Never underestimate the power of your attitude. How you handle difficult situations will be a direct result of how you view things.

After all your expertise, your huffing and puffing, your successes and your failures, all you have left is your attitude towards how you will handle the next day or the next crisis.

This being the case, you need to make sure you are constantly checking your attitude to ensure it's on track.

Remember: if you are just going through life waiting to see what it will bring you, then you just have to be prepared to accept whatever comes your way. Good or bad.

Or you can make your life head the way you want it to go.

The slogan says it all!

Introduction

When I first started Attitude Gear® I had the great idea of put[ting]
slogans on the back of t-shirts. I never thought that one simple [idea]
would reach the heights that it did and still does today.

While there are a lot of slogans and sayings out there, I want[ed to]
have a range of positive—and sometimes sarcastic—slogans that [any]
one would be prepared to wear to show who they are.

Sometimes when things are tough we wish we could just s[tay in]
bed. So we all need to constantly remind ourselves why we g[et out]
of bed every day.

This book is designed for you to read not only when thing[s aren't]
going as planned, but also when everything is working just pe[rfectly.]

There is no finish line in life. Just because you achieve '[success']
before others around you, does not mean that you have reache[d a level]
of importance above everyone else.

We are all placed on this planet to excel.

I hope you will get enjoyment out of these slogans, b[ut more]
importantly, I hope you take in the messages behind them a[nd ...]

IN THE END IT'S ALL A MATTER OF ATTITUDE

These days, wanting to be better is too often seen as a negative thing. The whole 'tall poppy' syndrome is well and truly alive.

Dare to be better, not in a way that is competitive for competitiveness sake with those around you, but more aimed at yourself.

Dare to better the results you have already achieved. Issue yourself a challenge to lift your expected outcomes. Never compare yourself to others and their results. All you then really set yourself up for are their outcomes. In the end other people's outcomes may be nowhere near where you want to be.

Challenge yourself every morning when you wake up. Try to better the outcomes you got the previous day. Not in a striving and painful way, but more in a way that keeps you fired-up and motivated.

As my father always said when I was a kid, 'If you aim at nothing, you will hit it every time'.

Constantly remind yourself that you are better than the outcomes that you experience. This doesn't mean you are better than everyone else, it just means you are constantly bettering yourself. Big difference really!

I DON'T CARE HOW GOOD YOU ARE . . . I'M BETTER!

It's all a matter of attitude

Are you aiming to win? By this I mean, do you want to complete everything you do with a sense of total satisfaction because you know that you have put in 100 per cent?

Never settle for second best. Never start something if you know that you won't be bothered if you never finish it.

Excellence is a learnt skill. Once you learn and apply it, you will find it hard to go back to being mediocre. The feeling you get when you win something—whether it was a race when you were at school, a competition or even a business award—is so worth the extra effort that is needed to win.

Believing that you are a winner is a great attitude to have; when things don't work out the way you have planned, they won't really slow you down because you will just bounce back and start all over again.

Remember though, even if some things don't work out as planned, you can still get back on track. It all comes down to the way that you perceive a setback. It's all about your mindset.

I'M IN THE BUSINESS OF WINNING AND BUSINESS IS GOOD

It's all a matter of attitude

I have met many people over the years who have no ambition to succeed. They don't care if they fail; in fact it seems as though they are actually planning for failure.

Losing should never enter your thoughts. The minute it does it sows an area of doubt that, if not addressed, can grow and bring undone the biggest of dreams and all of the potential in the world.

Don't plan for failure, plan for the great things that will happen due to your focus. Sure, there will be tough times, but never see yourself losing your grip on your future.

If you remove the thought of losing from your head, then no matter how many times you hit a hurdle along your journey, you will still get back on track. This attitude towards success becomes second nature.

Just because something doesn't work out for you, never think that you are a loser. All it means is that it is going to take you a little bit longer to achieve your goals.

You see, it's all about how you view it really.

LOSING IS NOT AN OPTION

Unfortunately, despite what some people think, success doesn't 'just happen'. And it doesn't select who it will and won't affect. You will have to make your success yours. You need to own your success and all that it entails.

The people I've met who would be considered very successful were not handed success on a platter. They all had to work at it, and very hard at that. They understood the principle that either they made their success or life would just happen to them.

What are you prepared to live with?

Will you just accept whatever you are dealt, or are you going to make success with anything and everything inside you?

Never be in a position where you have things happening to you. Be in control and direct your future. Don't let your life happen around you. Achieving is all about controlling the final outcome.

Make your successes happen. It really is up to you.

WINNERS MAKE IT HAPPEN . . . LOSERS LET IT HAPPEN

It's all a matter of attitude

Recently I watched my eldest daughter, Jade, play in an indoor soccer match. She was new to the sport but after watching a few games on television she knew one thing for sure: if you lose control of the ball, the potential outcomes may not be in your favour. She played so well that day. She was in control, so much so that she was the best player on the court.

Just like Jade and her soccer game, make sure you are always in control of your goals, dreams and life. The minute you let that control be taken from you is the minute your outcomes are in the hands of others.

Never hand over control of your goals and dreams to anyone else. If you do, you will have to be happy with the results that they bring you. Good or bad.

Just like taking your hands off the wheel of a car, your life and direction can quickly go astray if not closely monitored.

Make controlling your outcomes a top priority.

WHEN YOU CONTROL THE BALL YOU CONTROL THE SCORE

It's all a matter of attitude

I can't stand it when people come out with the old line, 'Well, if you want my opinion . . .

I'm not sure about you but I am sick and tired of people giving me their opinion on how I should live my life or run different parts of it, when they themselves aren't kicking any of their own goals.

The number of people who tried to give me their opinion when I started my first business was amazing. Had I listened to most of that advice, I doubt I would've ended up where I have.

Be very selective about who you will and won't listen to and who you allow to give you their opinion. Odds are the opinions won't be great, and these people won't stick around to help you pick up the pieces either.

There is nothing wrong with asking for advice. But I suggest you ask people who have achieved a level of success in your desired field.

WHEN I WANT YOUR OPINION, I'LL GIVE IT TO YOU!

It's all a matter of attitude

If you have read any of my other books, you will understand my dislike for people who constantly play the 'blame game'. There is nothing worse than being surrounded by these types of people.

Making excuses for where you are in your life right now will not change a thing.

The only thing that will is getting off your butt and doing something different.

I remember my father referring to people who give up as those who have 'loser's limp'. You know when you were a kid and you were playing a game and winning, then all of a sudden your opponent 'hurts' themselves and has to retire?

Anyone can make excuses. In fact it is easier to excuse your failings and your shortcomings than it is to admit you have them.

The day that you take ownership of your shortcomings is the day those excuses will stop. It is up to you to stop the excuses and start the successes.

EXCUSES ARE FOR LOSERS

LOSERS

It's all a matter of attitude

Anyone who has read my other books will understand the importance I place on change.

Too often we try to achieve new tasks or aim at new goals while all the time thinking we can achieve them by staying the same.

Unless you accept change in your life, you will continually get the same results. That's fine if you are happy with the results you have been getting. I'm not sure about you, but I want to better my outcomes every time I aim for something new.

What changes do you have to make?

What areas have you left unchanged for a while that are slowing you down?

It is usually the simple, easy things that require change. This being the case, just think how much of an impact these simple changes will make.

As the old saying goes, 'Change is as good as a holiday'.

IF NOTHING CHANGES . . . NOTHING CHANGES!

It's all a matter of attitude

While there is a touch of humour to this slogan there is also a lot of common sense. When I came up with it I was trying to emphasise the importance of both leadership and ownership.

The minute you allow others to take over your direction is the minute you are at the mercy of their outcome.

There is nothing wrong with wanting people around you to enjoy and experience your journey through life. But never forget that it is you who is in the driver's seat.

I don't believe leaders are made. Sure, you can teach someone the elements of leadership, but some people are just born leaders. So why let others steal the leadership with regards to your own aspirations?

True leaders will always have people following them. Make sure you lead them to a place they need to go. There is nothing better than having people around you who are grateful for what you have done for them.

Own the process of your success. Some of you may need to start the process for others as well. That is what being a leader is all about.

LET'S WORK AS A TEAM AND DO IT MY WAY!

It's all a matter of attitude

It's all a matter of attitude

This slogan has special meaning for me. I printed it on a t-shirt and sent it to the lady who continually told me I had an attitude problem. While I got a lot of satisfaction out of doing this, the fact is the statement is very true.

People will always have an opinion or perception of who you are, what you are doing wrong and even the issues you need to face. When you start allowing other people's perceptions to become fact in your life, you start marching to their beat.

The best way to overcome other people's perceptions is to constantly keep your own attitudes in check. If you know you are headed in the right direction, then what other people say to you will have no impact on your journey.

Don't allow other people—who most probably have got bigger issues themselves—to disrupt where you want to go.

I DON'T HAVE AN ATTITUDE PROBLEM . . . YOU HAVE A PERCEPTION PROBLEM

It's all a matter of attitude

I was with my eldest daughter at a video store one day when I noticed a large group of young males acting tough to passers-by. It dawned on me that there are some people out there trying so hard to be something that they are not.

Sure, you can do courses on many things to improve your life, but ultimately it is up to you to use what you've got.

Too many people think there are secrets out there on how to live a better life, how to make more money, even how to have successful relationships. Well I am going to let you know the most important secret: JUST DO IT!

We all have within us the secrets to all of our quests. The fact is we need to unlock those secrets by understanding who we are and where we are falling short.

Your 'attitude' towards this task will determine your outcome.

SOME WORK AT IT, SOME FAKE IT, SOME EVEN DO COURSES ON IT, BUT ME . . . I WAS JUST BORN WITH IT

It's all a matter of attitude

This slogan has been around for many years but still has impact.

I can't stand it when people apply the least amount of effort to their lives only to then whinge and complain that nothing ever works out for them.

You need to make sure that, whatever you decide to start, you are prepared for a long haul. Nothing comes easy for anyone. If you are not prepared to go hard and put in the extra effort, then my advice to you is don't even bother starting. All you will do is frustrate yourself down the track and blame everyone around you for your failures.

Whatever you set your mind to, whether it be a personal or a work issue, make sure you attempt it with total focus and an understanding that 100 per cent effort is required.

You will be surprised by how easy it is to get distracted. If this does happen and some of your attention is elsewhere, you lessen your focus on achieving the goals you originally set for yourself.

Remember: if you stay focused on your desired outcome and apply 100 per cent effort, your dreams will become reality.

GO HARD OR JUST GO HOME

It's all a matter of attitude

I can't stand it when people say that if you are not living on the edge, you aren't living at all. What a stupid way to live. When you live on the edge, or by the seat of your pants, there is way too much room for error.

Sure, when you start something off, let's say a business, you really are flying blind. Any wrong turn or wrong decision can result in failure. If you've been there, you'll know that you never want to go back to that place.

So you need to understand that there is a whole lot more room out there where it is safer for you to operate.

There is nothing wrong with living a 'safe' life. In fact, the safer you feel within yourself and with what you are doing, the better you can concentrate on achieving all you desire.

Don't be a one-hit wonder. Don't think that you have to live on the edge all the time. Enjoy yourself and all that life brings.

THE EDGE IS NOT THE LIMIT . . . IT'S ONLY THE STARTING POINT

It's all a matter of attitude

I was watching a local rugby league match recently and the team I supported were being beaten hands down.

It was half-time and the score was 50–0. The losing team knew they were being beaten but up until that stage they didn't know by how much. When the coach told them the actual score, you could see the disappointment on all of their faces.

The coach tried to 'rev' them up before sending them back on the field. But, from a spectators' perspective, it seemed like a waste of time; the team had already given up. The final score was 82–0.

The minute you allow a losing attitude to enter your thinking, is the minute you allow a second outcome.

As humans we find it easier to focus on the negative rather than the positive. This being the case, ensure you keep your mind filled with the positive things around you.

If you can't seem to find any positives, then look harder. You will find that even the smallest things that are positive will make a huge difference to your outlook.

IF YOU THINK YOU'RE BEATEN ... YOU ARE!

Well this says it all really!

At some point, almost all of us will experience some type of a hiccup in life. For some it will be a small setback while for others it will be a huge setback.

Not everything is going to go according to how we originally planned it. So are you going to 'drop your bundle' or, in other words, just give up every time something doesn't work out as you envisioned it?

Odds are there is someone out there who is worse off than yourself.

Don't join the 'pity party' or dwell in the land of the self-wallowing. Just get on with getting on, in spite of the setbacks that cross your path.

As my father always used to say, 'When life hands you a lemon . . . make lemonade'.

Have an attitude that you CAN and WILL face whatever is thrown at you along your journey towards a successful life.

Just imagine not achieving anything for the rest of your life. Hmm . . . seems succeeding is a better way to go hey?

LIFE'S TOUGH . . .
SO WHAT!

Have a look at any world champion. The results they are currently achieving, or have already achieved, all started as just a dream. They didn't wake up one morning and decide they had nothing better to do than become a champion; each of them had a long and painful—but rewarding—journey.

You see, there are many people who look at what champions are achieving and say to themselves, 'They're just lucky, I'd like to experience that as well'.

Chances are that it has taken a lot of extra effort and a whole lot of focusing on their original dreams. It is unlikely they won the first race or event they entered. They would have experienced defeat along the way to the top. All they had to keep them going was the dream to succeed and to be the best.

What dreams have you had over the years but never acted on? What will it take for you to start on your journey towards realising those dreams?

There is no one more qualified to make your own dreams come true than yourself.

THE ONLY THING CHAMPIONS HAVE IN COMMON ARE THEIR DREAMS

It's all a matter of attitude

One thing I can't stand is people who constantly complain and whinge. You probably know the type I'm referring to: no matter what happens in their life, good or bad, they complain that 'nothing good ever happens to them'. After a while you just stop caring.

When you personally experience some success, the whingers again complain—but now they complain about your success and how it's just not fair that they 'never get the lucky breaks'.

After a while the last thing you want to do is associate yourself with them, as all they do is bring you down to their level.

While this slogan is a bit harsh, it's true that eventually you just stop caring because of the constant complaining and the constant negativity.

Don't be one of these people. Don't allow yourself to become negative. It is up to you to control your destiny and ultimately it is up to you to control whether you're affecting people in a positive or a negative way.

We all need a great support network around us—not just to receive what we want to hear; sometimes we also need to hear what we may not really like.

Don't—by being negative—separate yourself from the people around you.

TELL SOMEONE WHO CARES!

It's all a matter of attitude

Some people think that when they experience a certain level of success, they will suddenly become enthusiastic about what they are trying to achieve.

This is such a wrong way to think.

Our thinking is the key to unlocking a lot of our success. If we allow ourselves to be controlled by our negative thoughts, our actions will mirror this negativity.

I have always been enthusiastic about where I want to go in life.

Being positive doesn't mean that everything will always work out the way you plan, but it will help to keep you going in the right direction.

Don't surround yourself with negative people. Have people around you who are enthusiastic about their own success. Then, by default, you will follow their example and be forced along a positive path.

If setbacks come your way, be as enthusiastic about getting back on track as you would be if things were all falling into place.

This will force your thinking and actions back on the road to success.

GET ENTHUSIASTIC OR GET OUT OF MY FACE

It's all a matter of attitude

Success doesn't come easy or overnight.

The number of people I have met who are expecting to just coast through their lives while also aiming at some level of success is amazing. I have also met a lot of people who have given up after hitting a hurdle or problem.

The true test of a successful person, I believe, is not measured by their ultimate outcome but more by how many times they picked themselves up, dusted themselves off and got back on track.

You see it's all about the falls and the issues we face.

Few things irritate me more than people who have been handed success. Not because I am jealous—far from it. It is more that these people often seem to think they are better than others because they didn't do any work to get to where they are.

While some things may work out easier than others, it still comes down to pushing through barriers. If you stumble along your journey, don't dwell on the fall. Focus on getting back to where you were and learn from your mistakes.

Remember: success is all about the journey.

IT'S NOT WHETHER YOU GET KNOCKED DOWN . . . IT'S WHETHER YOU GET BACK UP

100% ATTITUDE . . . YOU GOT A PROBLEM WITH THAT?

It's all a matter of attitude

There is a lot to be said for visualising your success. Now I'm not getting all freaky on you here: I'm talking about having a clear picture in your head of what you would like to achieve.

I can guarantee that if you ask an Olympic gold medal winner whether they had just turned up on the day and hoped for the best, the answer would be no. When they are at the starting line, they are already picturing themselves finishing first. The fact is, only one person can win the race. Skill and strength will play a role, but the winner's attitude will be the deciding factor.

Many of you reading this book may not yet have made it to where you want to be. Don't let that stop you thinking like a champion.

I promise that if you begin to change your thinking and start acting like a champion, your results will soon follow.

TO BE A CHAMPION YOU HAVE TO BE THE BEST; IF YOU'RE NOT THEN JUST PRETEND YOU ARE

It's all a matter of attitude

Do you have a 'whatever it takes' attitude?

Are you prepared to fight tooth and nail to achieve whatever goals you have set for yourself?

There is no right or wrong way to achieve and reach the goals and dreams you have set for yourself.

I can't stand it when I see an ad in a magazine or newspaper for another seminar on the 'secrets to success'. What a load of garbage. There are no 'secrets'. There is only hard work, determination and desire.

This being the case, what are you prepared to go through to get where you want to go?

You need to have the right attitude to push through the difficulties and do whatever it takes to succeed. Why not look at simple ways to start? By that I mean don't get caught up thinking you have to understand everything you're about to get into.

I had absolutely no idea what I was doing when I started my business and I personally think that was the key to my early success. It was the simple things that made the biggest impact on my business growth. I did whatever it took to get myself out of the financial situation I was in.

What are you prepared to do to get to where you want to go?

WHATEVER IT TAKES!

It's all a matter of attitude

There are so many people waiting for the 'right time' to start something, whether that's a business, a new goal or even a diet.

Some people don't start anything because they want a guarantee that whatever they do start will result in the outcome they have envisioned. Guaranteed!

Well the fact is, there are no guarantees. So my advice is to JUST START! Even the smallest positive result is better than no result at all.

It would be wonderful, in this world of technology, if we could get an email informing us that today is the right day for us to succeed—but that isn't going to happen. The day you start will be the day you are on the road to succeeding.

It is all too easy to be negative. We are constantly surrounded by negativity. Just open any newspaper, watch or listen to any news bulletin and you will understand what I mean.

If we were to focus only on the reasons *why* we should attempt anything then none of us would achieve.

Focus on the positives and watch your world and outcomes change in front of you.

A POSITIVE ANYTHING IS BETTER THAN A NEGATIVE NOTHING

It's all a matter of attitude

Each and every one of us has control over where we will end up in our own lives.

Our journey towards success and happiness is exactly that—OURS!

You are the one behind the steering wheel. If you choose to hand over control of where you want to end up in your own life, then you will have to be prepared for whatever destination you arrive at.

I am not a great horse person, so if this next example doesn't make a great deal of sense then you will have to excuse me. When I was a lot younger I was invited to go horse riding. I thought I was going to have a nice relaxing day. How wrong was I! I was put on a 'very calm and placid' horse and off we all went.

After a while of nothing really happening, I decided to just let the reigns go and be a passenger. BANG! Something startled the horse and off it went with me holding onto the saddle for grim life. I had absolutely no control over that animal and I ended up on my backside.

A lot of people take the same approach throughout their lives; they only want to control the spoils of success and don't really care about the mundane issues and small things along the way.

If you lose control you will have no one but yourself to blame if you end up on your backside.

HE WHO LOSES CONTROL . . . LOSES

It's all a matter of attitude

Some of you will read this slogan and understand exactly where I'm coming from.

You may be surrounded by people who you just don't click with any more, even though they are trying to achieve all that they desire. This is not because you are better than them; it may just be that you are operating on a totally different personal and spiritual level.

I have had many friends over the years, but I look back today and there are only a handful who I see on a regular basis. Our lives have moved in different directions. Some are only worried about chasing the almighty dollar, which has never been my top priority. Others are waiting for 'something good' to happen to them before they start on their journey.

Make sure you surround yourself with like-minded people. I'm not talking about people who sing your praises every day; I'm talking about people who challenge you to achieve greater things.

JUST BECAUSE WE'RE ON THE SAME PLANET, DOESN'T MEAN WE'RE FROM THE SAME WORLD

It's all a matter of attitude

know some of you may be thinking, 'What a negative statement'. Really think about it before you comment though.

Too many people go through life with a victim mentality, so much so that they could make a lot of money out of being professional 'give-uperas' (no, you won't find that in the dictionary).

Others are just as happy to go through life blaming others, blaming their past and blaming those around them—all because they have failed to achieve anything they wanted to achieve. They end up becoming professional losers. They love the fact they never achieve because it then gives them an excuse they can use later on. They think people around them will continually feel sorry for them and that they can play the victim game for the rest of their lives.

I personally know of someone just like this. He is continually crying poor. He constantly tells others just how 'lucky' they have been, and that if he was as lucky, he'd be just as successful.

You see he has failed to realise that it is his attitude and mentality towards success that is keeping him where he is today.

Even if you are not yet where you want to be in life, never allow your thinking to become stuck in 'loser' mode.

SHOW ME A 'GOOD' LOSER AND I'LL SHOW YOU A LOSER!

It's all a matter of attitude

If you are reading this book and you have experienced a level of success, you will understand that you had to take risks along your journey.

There are a lot of people who freak out when they realise they need to take a risk. For example, I was speaking at a conference recently when a lady came up to me as I was signing my books. She started off with a statement that really summed up where she was at in her life, and why. She said, 'I want it all but I want it to be easy'. WOULDN'T WE ALL!!!!

I have a totally different view of risks and dramas. I love it when things aren't working out as planned. I love it when I need to take risks. It really forces me to lift my game and operate on a completely new level.

I was asked the other day by a journalist whether I was a 'glass half full' or 'glass half empty' type of person. My answer was simple: all I see is a glass—it is up to me to either fill it or empty it with my decisions.

Risks are just part of the process with regards to success. How you handle them will be determined by how you view them from the start.

IT IS THE RISK
THAT IS THE RUSH

It's all a matter of attitude

Our thinking plays such a huge role in how we operate on a daily basis. More so than a lot of people realise.

There are many people who will never experience the joys of success, all because they have already decided that success is going to be too hard for them and that it is only there for a few lucky people.

What are the areas in your life in which you think you can't achieve? What part of your thinking is allowing your actions to be restricted?

I sat next to a man on a plane not long ago and his first words to me were, 'I will never be able to experience the same level of success as you have'. You know, he is exactly right. He never will. Not because I am any better or smarter than he is. But because he has already made up his mind. His thinking will control his actions, which in turn will control his outcomes. His mindset has determined his end result.

Don't fall into the trap of focusing on why you won't be able to achieve. Be like one of those karate experts who break wood with their bare hands. Look past problems and break straight through them.

IF YOU THINK YOU CAN'T . . . YOU WON'T

It's all a matter of attitude

Oh he just got lucky'. Sound familiar?

People try to justify their own shortcoming by downplaying other people's successes.

I'm sure there was some luck involved in my business success, but luck comes and goes. I managed to turn that 'luck' into greater opportunities.

Often the biggest problem with success is how other people view it. They have no idea how hard you have worked to get to where you are today. All they see is the finished result. You and I know what was involved: the hard work, the disappointment and the long hours—only for something to fall over so you have to start again.

It is all too easy for those who haven't experienced any of this to sit and cast their opinions on other people's success. So easy, in fact, that it becomes part of who they are. You or I are never going to change them or the way they view success. That, I'm afraid, has to come from within themselves. The only thing we can do is make sure we don't become like them.

IT'S ALL ABOUT LUCK . . . JUST ASK ANY LOSER

I used to be one of those people who worried constantly about what others thought of me. Not only when I was struggling before I started my business, but also after I experienced some success.

A lot of you will totally understand where I am coming from with this. Many of us listen to what others say about us. But the funny thing is we never seem to take on the nice things that people say, only the negatives.

We all need to block our ears to negative people. I am sure there are some people who don't like what I have become. But if I were to open myself up to their comments, all I would be doing is allowing my direction, thoughts and actions to be dictated by people who really have no understanding of where I want to go in life.

If you have people around you who only seem to offer negativity, separate yourself from them and their comments.

Become bulletproof.

IT'S NONE OF MY BUSINESS WHAT YOU THINK OF ME!

I am sure each and every person reading this book can look back on their lives and find areas or decisions that they would rather have handled a different way.

If you focus on past mistakes or errors, they will resurface in your present. After experiencing a few setbacks early on in my business, I decided I would stop myself from regretting my mistakes. I have to say that this process really has helped me get to where I am today.

Don't focus on what you have done wrong. Focus on what you can do right.

The word 'regret' has a negative tone and can sometimes bring up a negative thought.

The fact is, we can't go back and change the past, but we can influence the future.

The other day I was sitting in traffic and I noticed the lady in the car next to me looking in her rear-vision mirror. So much so, she didn't realise she was creeping forward. Then it happened; she ran into the back of the car in front of her.

She was so busy looking behind her that she didn't see what was in front.

Unfortunately that's how a lot of people go through their lives. They are too worried about their past and their regrets to see that they can change their situation by focusing on tomorrow.

Never regret your past—just use it as a teacher for your future.

NO REGRETS . . . NOT EVEN A LITTLE ONE

It's all a matter of attitude

Talk is cheap. Actions speak louder than words.

These are sayings that you have probably heard a thousand times.

In today's world, where everyone is trying to achieve and reach success, I have noticed that there seem to be a lot more people out there just talking the talk instead of walking the walk and living their dreams.

You probably know the saying: 'Practise what you preach'. Well I have my own slant on that one. I preach what I practise. There's a bit of a difference.

It is up to you to be someone whose life speaks for itself. We all need to let our actions show who we are.

Be a person whose life is an example to all who come in contact with you.

Don't get caught up in the world of show and hype. Have a level of substance to everything that you do and all that you are.

DON'T TELL ME WHAT YOU'VE DONE . . . SHOW ME WHAT YOU CAN DO

It's all a matter of attitude

I have a thirteen-year-old daughter. If you have ever played a game with someone her age you will understand where I got this slogan from.

Jade can't stand it when I beat her. Sometimes we have to sit and play until she wins. But do you know what? I love that quality within her. She wants to continue until she has mastered whatever she is doing.

Is that like you or do you give up too easily?

Are you prepared to stick things out no matter how tough they are or how long they may take?

Or do you just throw in the towel when things don't go exactly to plan?

In the game of life there really is no winner. We only compete with ourselves: our thinking and our goals and the dreams we have set.

We all need to have a game plan to guide us as we progress towards the goals we have set for ourselves.

Don't think you will be able to just cruise through life and reap rewards. Be prepared to play the game of your life.

Remember: quitters never win and winners never quit.

THE GAME ISN'T OVER UNTIL I WIN

It's all a matter of attitude

Out of all of the slogans I came up with for Attitude Gear®, this would have to be my favourite.

I have a tendency to just tune out when people are speaking garbage to me. On the outside it might look as if I'm listening, but it's a completely different story inside my head.

I am constantly bombarded by people who either ring or email me with their problems. While I appreciate that I have the opportunity to help them, the difficulty with a lot of these people is that they don't actually want help at all. All they are really after is someone to sympathise with them and share their pain.

Well, unfortunately they don't get that from me. As soon as I show them where I believe they are going wrong, they quickly end the conversation.

Who are you allowing to 'infect' you with their garbage on a regular basis? The more you allow, the more they will think they have the right to play a part in your life.

JUST BECAUSE I'M LISTENING, DOESN'T MEAN I CARE!

It's all a matter of attitude

Sometimes we look from the start of a new venture and all we see are the hurdles and the reasons why we shouldn't even bother.

Remember: not everything you try will always work.

There are no excuses in life. There are no limits as to how high you can go. If all we were to do is focus on the negative aspects of any new opportunity, none of us would ever start anything.

I know what some of you are already saying to yourself: 'What if I don't succeed?' or, 'But you don't know what I have been through'.

Let me put it to you another way.

What if, by not starting, you miss the one great opportunity that may get you to where you want to go?

Your attitude towards excuses will show you exactly where you are at on your journey. It doesn't matter where your starting point is, it ultimately comes down to how much you want the goals and dreams that you have set for yourself, to become reality.

NO LIMITS,
NO EXCUSES,
NO IFS,
NO BUTS . . .
JUST ATTITUDE

It's all a matter of attitude

A little while back someone came up to me after I finished speaking to ask me a question. It went something like this: 'You have been successful. What did you do differently from people who have failed in their attempt to reach success?'

My answer was an easy one: 'EVERYTHING.'

Your success will come when you decide to do everything it takes to reach it. There is no right way, but there is a wrong way. You will know if you are doing it wrong when you don't get any results.

Winners are out there putting in the long hours, concentrating on their goals and doing whatever it takes to get results. Losers just sit back and wait for everything to happen for them—without ever raising a sweat.

Be determined to be a winner in life. Have an attitude that says, 'I am in this for the long haul'.

Don't expect to reach your desired outcome within the first few weeks of starting. Like a farmer waiting for his crop to be ready for harvest, put in the time and effort and you will reap your rewards.

WINNERS DO WHAT LOSERS DON'T

It's all a matter of attitude

wrote about this next example in my last book, *What Are You Waiting For?*

The four-minute mile was broken by a man by the name of Roger Banister. Many people had tried to break the record before him, but without success.

Even though Banister had broken the four-minute mile, you'd think it would have continued to be a hard record to crack. But in fact, over fifty other runners broke the four-minute mark over the next year.

You see, the impossible is just an imaginary line drawn in the sand of all that you wish to achieve.

Why can't you start and run a very successful business without any previous training? I did.

Why can't you achieve all that you set your mind to? I did.

Does this make me any better than you? Simple answer: NO.

It just means that I saw that the impossible was possible. What are you going to see as possible now?

THE IMPOSSIBLE IS WHAT NOBODY CAN DO UNTIL SOMEBODY DOES IT

It's all a matter of attitude

I am always being asked to speak about the issue of focus. We are constantly distracted from our goals; we allow other things to take priority. Most of the time those other things are way off our course.

Most of us seem to focus on the problems more than the solutions.

I will keep saying it: reaching the goals you have set for yourself will not be easy. But it is the path less travelled that will take you to living out those dreams and goals.

It is so easy to focus on the reasons why you will never achieve, or on all of the issues that stand in your way. But when you use these as an excuse, they will end up actually being the things stopping you.

The thing is, every single person will, and has, come across obstacles. You are no different. The only difference is that successful people didn't focus on those obstacles. They used obstacles to make them stronger.

So what is your excuse?

OBSTACLES ARE WHAT YOU SEE WHEN YOU TAKE YOUR EYES OFF YOUR GOALS

It's all a matter of attitude

The number of people who change as soon as they reach a level of success continues to amaze me.

I really don't understand why this happens. I suppose they get caught up in the outward trappings of success and then think that they are on a level above everyone else.

The one thing I have made sure I do is stay the same person I was before I experienced success.

I am also astounded by the number of people who will stoop to underhanded tactics to achieve their goals and dreams. Integrity and ethics seem to be sadly disappearing from some people's lives.

I have certain beliefs and I am not going to change them on my journey towards success. If you have to 'sell your soul' or, to put it another way, compromise the essence of who you are, to reach success, then you need to ask yourself if it is actually worth it.

Stay true to who you are and true to your beliefs. Trust me: as soon as you stray from these, you will not enjoy your success nearly as much.

I WOULD RATHER BE DISLIKED FOR WHAT I AM THAN LIKED FOR WHAT I AM NOT

It's all a matter of attitude

If you are working your way towards achieving your goals and dreams then this slogan should be put up somewhere you will see it every day.

We all need to strive for excellence on a daily basis. Sadly, there are a lot of people who just sit back and wait for whatever comes their way.

I am yet to watch the Olympics, or any other sporting competition, where an athlete answers 'second place', when asked what result they would be happy with.

They all go out there to win.

Now obviously there is only one winner in a race, but it is their attitude and focus before the race, and when they are on the starting line, that is most important.

Be aware also that not everything is going to work out as planned. The key to continually getting back on your path is never allowing your setbacks to infiltrate your thinking.

Always see yourself achieving the dreams you have. If you fall short, at least you are closer to those goals than you were before you started.

NO ONE TRAINS FOR SECOND PLACE

It's all a matter of attitude

I remember going through school watching the 'in-crowd' making fun of those who preferred to study than to play up.

The whole area of excellence is one that needs to be addressed by all of us every day with regard to our own journey.

There still seem to be people who think that they will be able to achieve all they desire by staying the same and refusing to change.

You need to remember that you should never stop learning, you should never stop growing and you should never think that you have made it and there is nothing more for you to achieve.

I want to be better every day. By wanting that, I am making a conscious decision to try new things, learn new things and maybe even get rid of some of my old attitudes or actions that are actually keeping me back.

Being excellent is a choice. So is being mediocre.

BE DIFFERENT . . .
BE BETTER

It's all a matter of attitude

I am constantly approached by people, whether by email or in person, who come out with the old line, 'It is impossible for me to get to where I want to go in life'.

I find that so sad. In their heads they have all but given up on reaching all that they desire.

The difference between people who have achieved their goals and people who haven't is that successful people see 'impossible' as 'possible'.

Impossible really is just an opinion. There is nothing set in stone to say that you will never achieve what you want. It is all up to you.

You might look at what you want to do but not be able to see a clear path towards success. It is all about looking at your journey from various directions.

I always think and operate from outside the square, so I am able to approach things in a new and fresh way.

On the outside it may look as though it will be impossible for you to start that business, get that promotion, go on that holiday or even buy that new car. But it is all up to whether you surrender yourself to that line of thinking, or whether you just ignore it and keep aiming to achieve everything in spite of it.

IMPOSSIBLE IS
JUST AN OPINION

It's all a matter of attitude

Be prepared for some pain along the way to achieving your successes. Too many people think that everything is going to go smoothly and then get a rude awakening when they hit a hurdle.

You are going to have to stretch yourself, do things that you have never attempted before and maybe even separate yourself from friends and attitudes, just to get to where you want to go.

You don't seriously think that you can go through all of this without feeling some type of mental discomfort, do you?

The good news is that pain will go away and you will end up a better and stronger person for it.

Just as many of us experienced growing pains when we were children, the same applies for growing into our goals.

The reason you haven't reach those goals is because you have yet to go through things that will bring you closer to them.

Don't give up because you don't want to face those changes. Tackle them head on and watch yourself grow.

A LITTLE BIT OF PAIN NEVER REALLY HURT ANYONE

It's all a matter of attitude

What are you focusing on? The excuses as to why you will never succeed or the reasons as to why you just have to?

I know that this slogan may seem simple but really look at it.

Too many people focus on the wrong areas, maybe even the areas where they are strongest, and forget their weak spots.

In my business, I never focused on the areas where I was doing well. You know why? Because I was already good at them. I focused all of my attention on the areas that I needed to improve. I had to make myself stronger in those areas. Then I would be better equipped to tackle my future head on.

If all you see are the dramas and reasons why you will never succeed, then start lifting your focus higher. Change your focus to areas that will give you results sooner.

You may be making only small gains, but at least you are going in a forward direction.

IN LIFE, WHAT YOU FOCUS ON IS ALL THAT YOU WILL SEE

It's all a matter of attitude

Never, never, never give up. Those are the famous words that Sir Winston Churchill gave at a school assembly.

I want to go through life continually amazing myself with my achievements and successes. I will never do that if I constantly quit.

There are too many quitters these days, people who just give up way too early.

I know a guy who starts a new business almost every week. He just hasn't learnt the whole principle of following through on what he starts. He has unfinished projects all over the place.

He gets so frustrated with people who have achieved success. So much so, that all he does is speak negatively about them. He is bitter about their victories. I believe that he is projecting his own thoughts about himself onto others.

When I first started Attitude Gear® I made a pact with myself which I called 'the no exit clause'. I was not going to allow myself to exit what I had started. No matter what happened along the way, I was determined to overcome it.

Why not set yourself a 'no exit' clause? Just promise yourself that you will never give up.

QUITTING IS A LOSER'S SHORTCUT

It's all a matter of attitude

I came up with this slogan because when I was starting out, I was constantly bombarded with negative comments from people who really had no idea. They were trying to force on me not only their attitudes towards my pending success but also their failures and their slant on how to achieve.

Depends who you ask, but I know my attitude was on-track right from the start.

I knew that I was sick and tired of not really being anywhere at the age of 25. Sure, I wanted a lot of nice things but the fact is, I was yet to experience any of them. It was up to me, and me alone, to get off my backside and start towards those goals.

If you have people around you whose attitude towards your success stinks, then you need to seriously think about removing yourself from them.

Remember, attitudes are contagious: both positive and negative. It is up to you to choose in which camp you are going to set up your tent every day.

I DON'T NEED YOUR ATTITUDE— I HAVE ONE OF MY OWN

It's all a matter of attitude

Yes I know, not the most positive slogan but I'll let you in on where it came from.

I was travelling to the airport when I had to stop at a set of traffic lights. After a little while another car pulled up beside me. The guy driving the car wound down his window and just started laying into me. He had something to say about my car, my bald head, my shirt—you name it, he had a go.

He said that it was people like me that made him sick by driving a nice car and thinking we are better than everyone else. I just turned around and came out with the statement on the opposite page.

You will undoubtedly come across people in life who, no matter what you do or say, will still have a problem with the world.

One of my favourite sayings is: 'You just can't please some people. If you give them a million dollars they will probably complain that it is too heavy to carry home.'

We can't please everybody we come across, and I am certainly not going to try to please people who really don't care.

Make sure you aren't one of those people who show the world how big the chip on their shoulder is.

If you want to make a lasting impression on people, make sure it is a positive one.

YOUR VILLAGE CALLED—THEIR IDIOT IS MISSING!

It's all a matter of attitude

This slogan was originally made for our series of motor sport t-shirts but I had another meaning behind it. I am a very simple person— not only on the outside but also with my thinking.

I have always thought and operated by using two areas: positive and negative. It really makes life a lot more simple.

That is why I absolutely love my role as a motivational speaker. Every time I am about to get up on stage, no matter where I am or to whom I am about to speak, the same thought runs through my head: 'I can either impact people in a positive way or a negative way.'

I encourage you to think like this the next time you meet up with someone. Even better, why not make that a conscious decision every day when you get out of bed.

The more simple you keep your life and your actions, the easier it will be to achieve all that you want to achieve.

I DREAM IN BLACK AND WHITE

It's all a matter of attitude

This is the only slogan in this book that did not make it onto an Attitude Gear® t-shirt.

I just wanted to end this book with a word of encouragement for everyone who has read it.

First, thank you so much for picking up this book.

Second, I urge you to live life well. It is so easy to get caught up in the 'doing' that we can easily miss the greatness of every day.

My youngest daughter is three years old. I am still amazed by how much pleasure she gives me just by doing the simplest things.

You see, while we are all trying to achieve everything we want out of life, it can be just as satisfying to spend time with your closest friends or to take your partner to the beach and have hot chips on the sand.

Keep your focus on where you want to go, but never lose sight of what is great around you right now.

I wish you all the best with all that you do and I pray that you experience success in every area of your life.